W9-DGA-815

JUN - - 2014

WITHDRAWN
Wo dridge Public Library

Anglerfish

by Ruth Owen

PowerKiDS
press.

New York

WOODRIDGE PUBLIC LIBRARY
3 PLAZA DRIVE
WOODRIDGE, IL 60517-5014
(630) 964-7899

Published in 2014 by The Rosen Publishing Group, Inc.
29 East 21st Street, New York, NY 10010

Copyright © 2014 by The Rosen Publishing Group, Inc.

All rights reserved. No part of this book may be reproduced in any form without permission in writing from the publisher, except by a reviewer.

Produced for Rosen by Ruby Tuesday Books Ltd
Editor for Ruby Tuesday Books Ltd: Mark J. Sachner
US Editor: Joshua Shadowens
Designer: Emma Randall

Photo Credits:
Cover, 1, 4–5, 6, 12–13, 16–17, 24–25 © Superstock; 7, 8–9, 10–11, 15, 19, 20–21, 22–23, 27 © FLPA; 28–29 © Shutterstock.

Library of Congress Cataloging-in-Publication Data

Owen, Ruth, 1967– author.
 Anglerfish / by Ruth Owen.
    pages cm. — (Real life sea monsters)
 Includes index.
 ISBN 978-1-4777-6257-8 (library) — ISBN 978-1-4777-6258-5 (pbk.) —
 ISBN 978-1-4777-6259-2 (6-pack)
 1. Anglerfishes—Juvenile literature. I. Title. II. Title: Anglerfish.
 QL637.9.L6O94 2014
 597'.62—dc23

                          2013028224

Manufactured in the United States of America

CPSIA Compliance Information: Batch #W14PK7: For Further Information contact: Rosen Publishing, New York, New York at 1-800-237-9932

CONTENTS

A Deadly Trap...4

Sea Monsters 6

Physical Facts 8

Gone Fishing..10

Bait That Glows 12

Dinner! 14

Looking for Love 16

Together Forever 18

Mom and Dad...20

Tiny Sea Monsters 22

The Humpback Anglerfish 24

Monkfish..26

Eating Sea Monster 28

Glossary...30

Websites...31

Read More..32

Index...32

A DEADLY TRAP

In a world of total darkness, a mile (km) beneath the surface of the ocean, a horrific monster is hunting for its next meal.

In this deep, dark part of the ocean, which is known as the midnight zone, the only clue that the beast is near is a tiny light above its head. A small fish spots the light and swims closer and closer, believing the light could be something to eat.

Suddenly, when it is much too late to escape, the fish sees the enormous mouth of vicious teeth waiting beneath the light. The little fish has just been **lured** to its death by a deadly, deep-sea **predator**, the anglerfish!

Light

An anglerfish

Anglerfish get
their name because, like
human anglers who catch fish
use fishing rods, these fish
use a fishing rod-like
body part to catch
other fish.

SEA MONSTERS

For hundreds of years, seafarers told stories of sea serpents and other strange beasts that lived in the world's oceans.

Today, we know these beasts do not exist, but many weird real-life sea monsters have been discovered, such as anglerfish. These fish are some of the most terrifying-looking creatures on Earth, and deserve the title of real-life sea monsters.

There are more than 200 different **species** of anglerfish. Many spend their lives swimming in open water. Others live their lives on the seabed. Sometimes, these bottom-dwelling anglerfish even walk about on the bottom of the ocean using their fins.

A deep-sea, open water anglerfish

A bottom-dwelling anglerfish

Anglerfish live in oceans all over the world.

PHYSICAL FACTS

Some species of anglerfish have their eyes on the sides of their heads. Others are flat fish that live on the seabed and have eyes on the tops of their heads.

Many species of anglerfish measure just a few inches (cm). Some species, however, grow to up to 3 feet (1 m) long.

Anglerfish have huge heads, and females have a body part known as a **lure** on their heads that they use for attracting **prey**. The lure is made up of a fleshy part called the **esca**, which is on the end of a long stem, or spine.

Some species of fish have bony skeletons, while others have skeletons made of tough, rubbery material called cartilage. All anglerfish have bony skeletons.

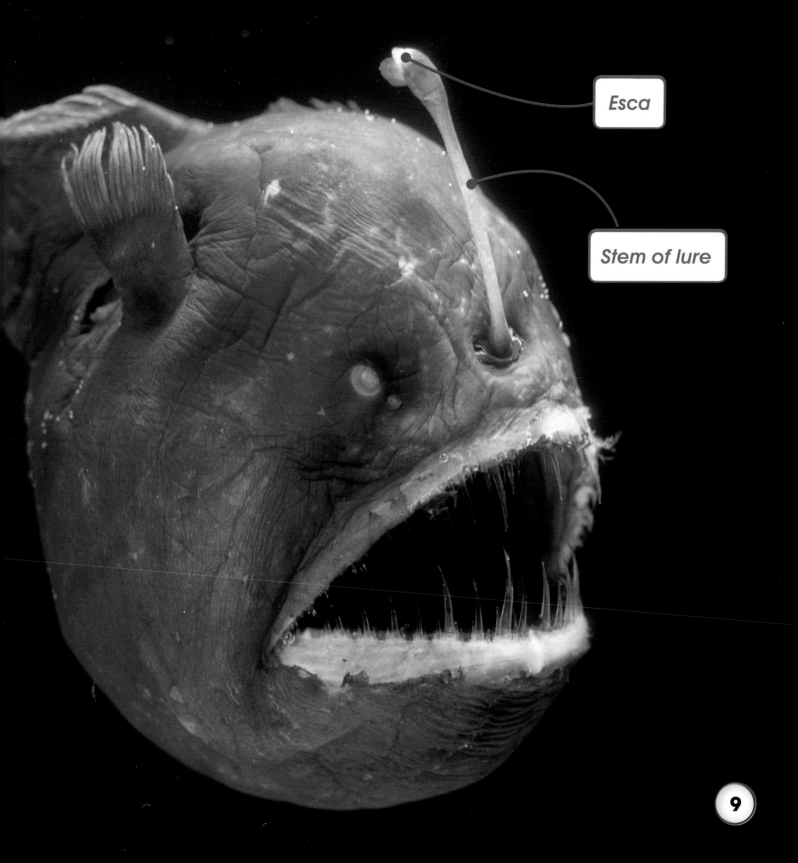

Esca

Stem of lure

GONE FISHING

The lures on the heads of anglerfish are actually spines like those found inside the fins on a fish's back. In anglerfish, the front spine has moved forward and **evolved** to become a fishing rod-like body part.

When an anglerfish's lure moves, the esca on the end of the spine wriggles and flutters in the water. Just as a human angler uses a worm to attract fish to a hook on the end of a line, the anglerfish uses its esca like bait.

Prey animals, such as other fish or squid, see the esca moving and think it's a tasty meal such as a shrimp. Once the prey animal gets close enough to the anglerfish to investigate the bait, it is doomed!

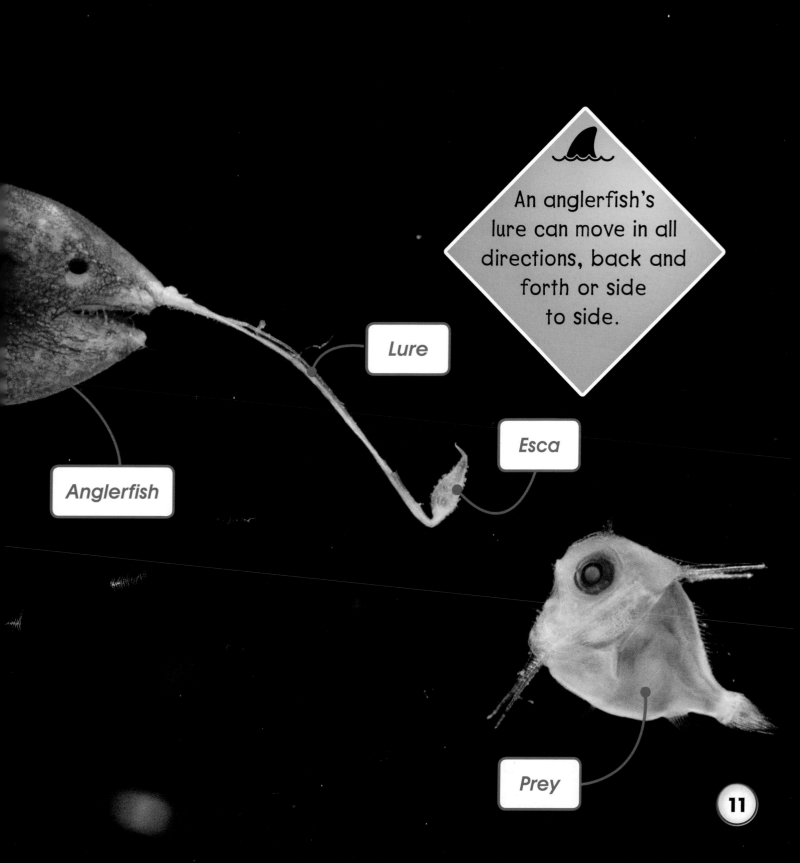

An anglerfish's lure can move in all directions, back and forth or side to side.

Lure

Esca

Anglerfish

Prey

BAIT THAT GLOWS

A lure is a successful way to attract prey. If you're a deep-sea anglerfish living in darkness, though, how will your prey even see the lure?

Many species of anglerfish have lures that actually glow! The light is created by **bacteria** that produce their own light.

Some scientists think the microscopic bacteria enter the fish's lure through pores, which are tiny openings in the skin. Once they are inside the lure, the bacteria form a partnership with the fish. The bacteria get **nutrients** from the fish, while the fish gets to use the bacteria's light to create glowing bait.

Glowing lure

Deep-sea anglerfish

When living things, such as bacteria, are able to create light, it is called bioluminescence.

DINNER!

Once a prey animal has been lured close to the anglerfish, the fish snatches its prey with its huge mouth.

An anglerfish's mouth is not only enormous, it is also able to open very wide. In fact, the fish's huge, gaping jaws are actually able to grab and then swallow creatures that are larger than the anglerfish!

An anglerfish's mouth is armed with many sharp teeth that often look as if they are made of glass. The teeth point slightly backward. This helps the prey slide more easily into the anglerfish. The position of the teeth also keep the victim from escaping the fish's jaws.

An anglerfish's stomach and body can stretch to hold a meal that is larger than the fish itself!

LOOKING FOR LOVE

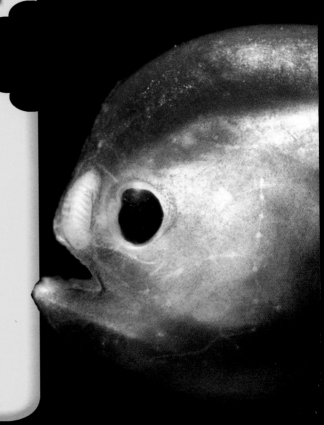

In deep, dark ocean waters it can be difficult to find and keep a **mate**. Male anglerfish, however, have developed ways to find and hold onto a female.

As soon as a male anglerfish is fully grown, he devotes his time to searching the ocean for a female. A male anglerfish has scent **organs** that he uses to sniff for females. He will keep swimming and swimming until he detects the scent of a female in the water.

Once the male finds a female, he bites into her belly and doesn't let go!

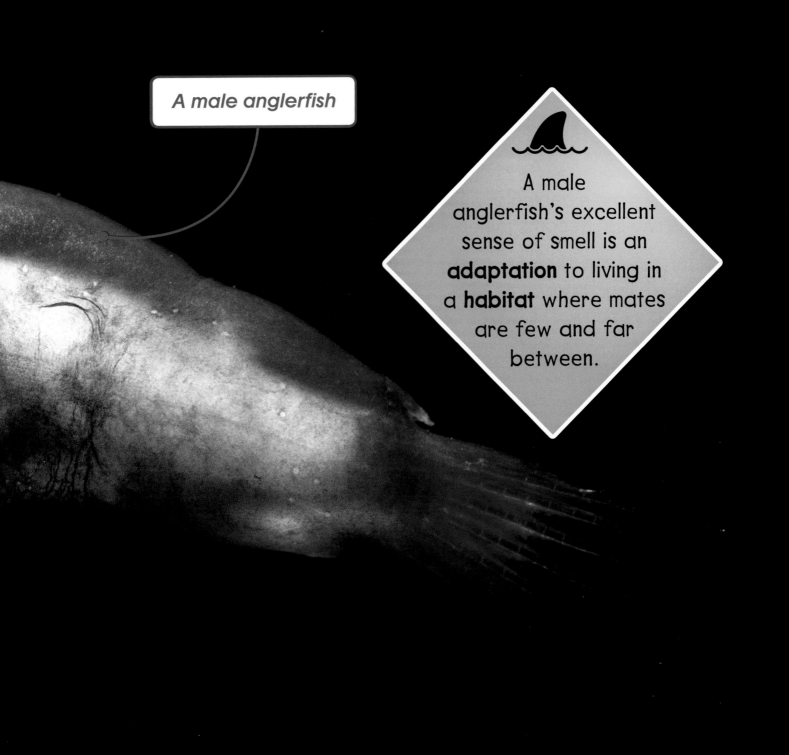

A male anglerfish

A male anglerfish's excellent sense of smell is an **adaptation** to living in a **habitat** where mates are few and far between.

TOGETHER FOREVER

Once a male anglerfish bites into his mate, the two fish become joined. Forever!

The male fish releases a substance from his mouth that dissolves his own mouth and the female's skin so the two fish **fuse** together. Now the male has actually become a part of his partner.

In time, the male loses his eyes and most of his organs, and his body shrivels. He gets the nutrients and **oxygen** he needs to survive from his partner. This is why only female anglerfish have lures. Adult males have no need to go fishing because they live off their mates!

Some male anglerfish have no digestive systems. They will starve unless they quickly attach to a female to get nutrients.

Male anglerfish

Female anglerfish's belly

MOM AND DAD

Once a male anglerfish is attached to his mate, his life as a free-swimming fish is over. In time, all that is left of the male fish are his body parts that are needed for reproduction.

Most female fish need to find a male fish to fertilize their eggs so that they can produce young. Once a male is attached to a female anglerfish, she has no need to do this. She can produce eggs and fertilize them using the male's body parts.

Sometimes, a female anglerfish may have as many as six different males attached to her body. She then produces young from all the males.

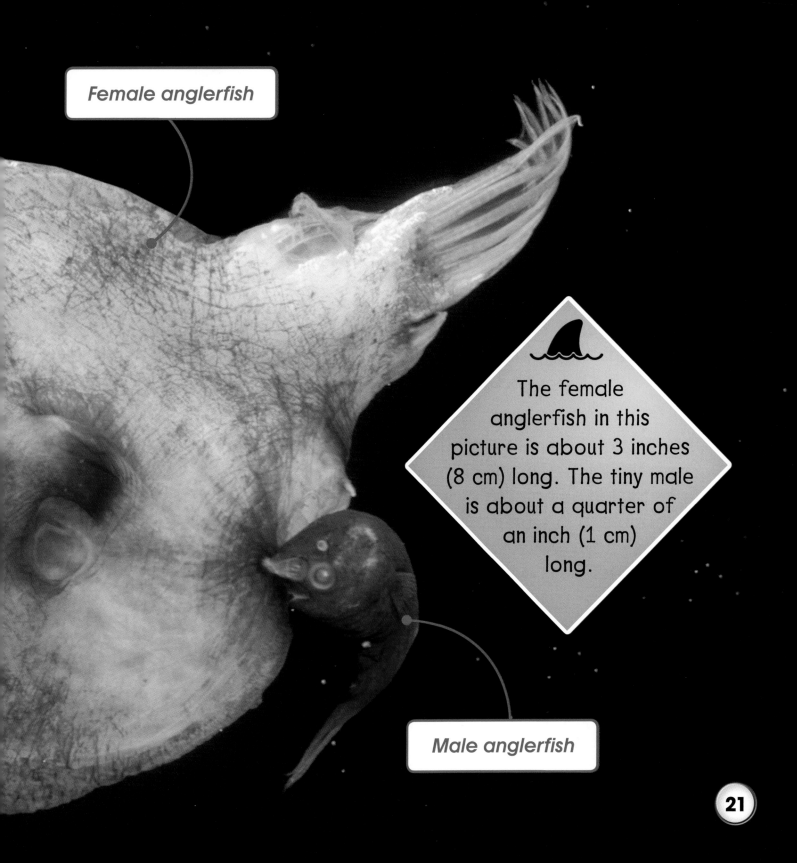

Female anglerfish

The female anglerfish in this picture is about 3 inches (8 cm) long. The tiny male is about a quarter of an inch (1 cm) long.

Male anglerfish

TINY SEA MONSTERS

Some species of anglerfish can produce millions of eggs at one time!

Some types lay their eggs inside a large sheet of slime. The slimy sheet can be 3 feet (1 m) wide and 33 feet (10 m) long! An anglerfish's eggs float to the surface of the water. Inside the eggs, baby fish called **larvae**, or fry, develop.

Scientists know very little about the lives of anglerfish larvae. They think, however, that once the larvae hatch, they live in open water close to the surface. They do this until they have grown large enough to dive deeper and begin hunting.

Anglerfish larvae probably feed on plankton, which are microscopic ocean creatures.

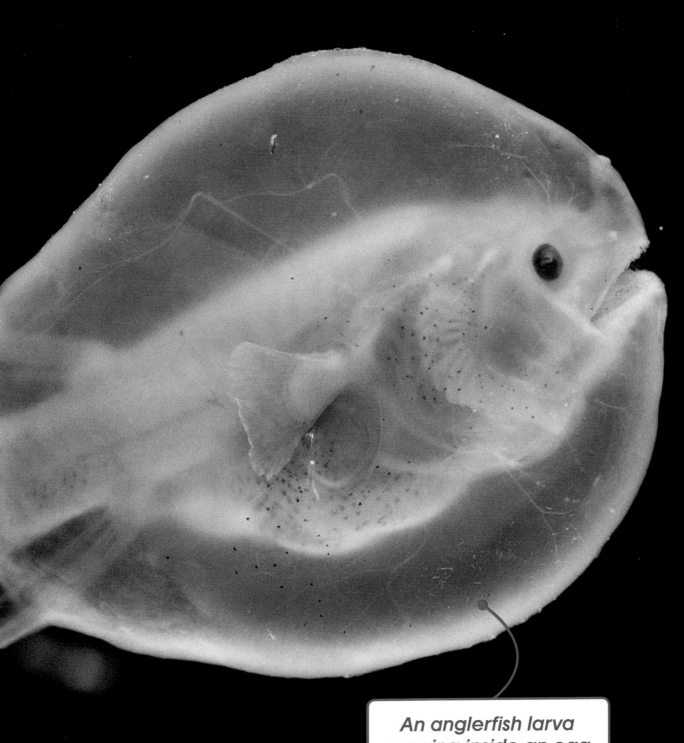

An anglerfish larva
growing inside an egg

THE HUMPBACK ANGLERFISH

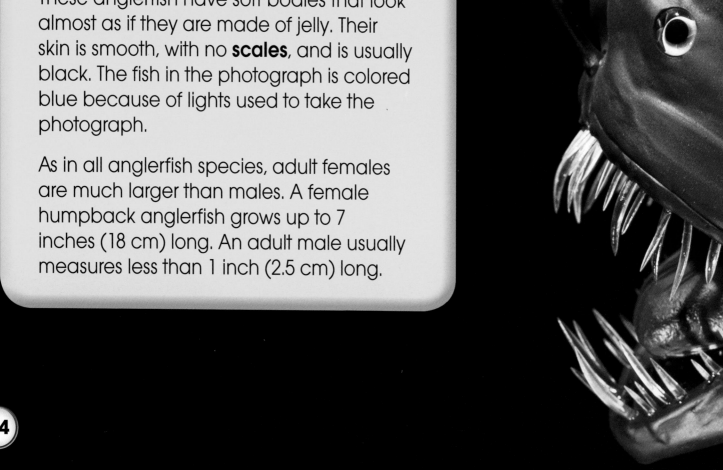

The humpback anglerfish lives in warm waters in the Pacific, Atlantic, and Indian Oceans. It is also known as the black seadevil.

These anglerfish have soft bodies that look almost as if they are made of jelly. Their skin is smooth, with no **scales**, and is usually black. The fish in the photograph is colored blue because of lights used to take the photograph.

As in all anglerfish species, adult females are much larger than males. A female humpback anglerfish grows up to 7 inches (18 cm) long. An adult male usually measures less than 1 inch (2.5 cm) long.

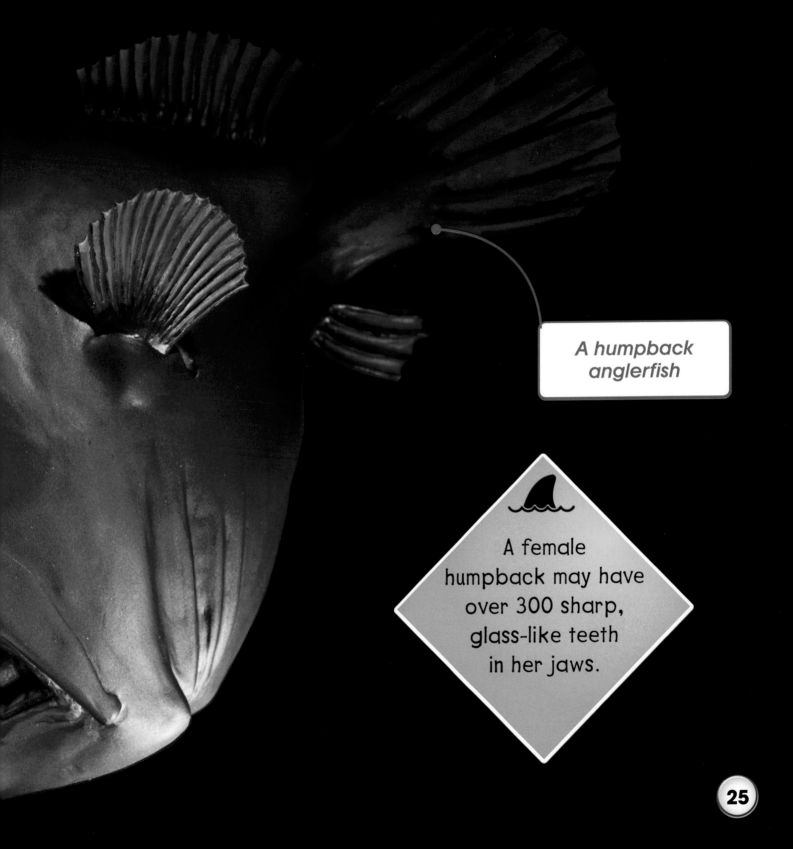

A humpback anglerfish

A female humpback may have over 300 sharp, glass-like teeth in her jaws.

MONKFISH

Some types of anglerfish are known by the common name of monkfish, or goosefish. These bottom-dwelling anglerfish spend their lives on the seabed.

When one of these large, flat fish goes hunting, it lies partially buried in mud or sand. Then it waves its lure through the water to attract its prey. When an unsuspecting victim gets near, the hidden hunter grabs its prey in its huge mouth.

An adult female monkfish may grow to be 6.5 feet (2 m) long. She can weigh over 80 pounds (36 kg). Males are much smaller at around 16 inches (41 cm) long.

Lure

A female monkfish, or goosefish, may live for 20 years or more.

Monkfish

Mouth

EATING SEA MONSTER

The weird-looking members of the anglerfish family known as monkfish, or goosefish, have enormous heads. They look as if they are all head and no body.

With their fierce, frightful faces and lumpy skin, monkfish don't look much like something you'd like to have appear on your dinner plate. This type of anglerfish, however, is a very popular fish for eating around the world, and often appears on menus in restaurants.

Just think. If you've ever eaten some juicy, white monkfish, you've eaten a real-life sea monster!

Most of the flesh that people eat when they eat monkfish is from the fish's tail.

A monkfish caught for food

Monkfish and tomato kebabs

GLOSSARY

adaptation (a-dap-TAY-shun)
A way in which a living thing's behavior or body has changed to make it better able to survive. Adaptations are passed on to the generations that come after.

bacteria (bak-TEER-ee-uh)
Tiny living things that can only be seen with a microscope. Some bacteria are helpful, while others are harmful.

esca (ES-kuh)
A fleshy growth at the end of a spine, or stem, on the head of an anglerfish.

evolved (ih-VOLVD)
Developed and changed gradually over many years.

fuse (FYOOZ)
To join and blend together.

habitat (HA-buh-tat)
The place where an animal or plant normally lives. A habitat may be a forest, the ocean, or a backyard.

larvae (LAHR-vee)
The young of some animals, including fish and insects.

lure (LOOR)
Something used to attract prey.

lured (LOORD)
Attracted by something that is wanted, such as food.

mate (MAYT)
To get together to produce young. Also, the word for an animal's partner with which it has young.

nutrients (NOO-tree-ents)
Substances that living things need to grow, get energy, and stay healthy.

organs (OR-gunz)
Body parts that have a particular important job to do.

oxygen (OK-sih-jen)
The gas that humans and other animals need to breathe.

predator (PREH-duh-tur)
An animal that hunts and kills other animals for food.

prey (PRAY)
An animal that is hunted by another animal as food.

scales (SKAYLZ)
Small, overlapping segments of skin. Fish and reptiles, such as snakes, have scales.

sea serpents (SEE SUR-pents)
Huge, ocean-dwelling monsters that appear in old stories. They were often described as having long, arm-like body parts called tentacles.

species (SPEE-sheez) One type of living thing. The members of a species look alike and can produce young together.

WEBSITES

Due to the changing nature of Internet links, PowerKids Press has developed an online list of websites related to the subject of this book. This site is updated regularly. Please use this link to access the list:

www.powerkidslinks.com/rlsm/angler/

READ MORE

Harrison, Paul. *Sea Monsters*. Up Close. New York: PowerKids Press, 2008.

Lynette, Rachel. *Deep-Sea Anglerfish and Other Fearsome Fish*. Creatures of the Deep. Mankato, MN: Capstone Press, 2012.

Niver, Heather Moore. *20 Fun Facts About Anglerfish*. Fun Fact File: Fierce Fish! New York: Gareth Stevens Learning Library, 2012.

INDEX

B
bacteria, 12–13
bioluminescence, 13
bottom-dwelling anglerfish, 6–7, 26–27
E
eating anglerfish, 28–29
eggs, 20, 22–23
escas, 8–11
F
female anglerfish, 8, 16, 18–21, 24–25, 27
H
humpback anglerfish, 24–25

hunting, 5, 8, 10–11, 22, 26
L
larvae, 22–23
lifespan, 27
lights (on anglerfish), 4–5, 12
lures, 8–12, 18, 26–27
M
male anglerfish, 16–17, 18–19, 20–21, 24
mates, 16–21
monkfish, 26–29
P
physical characteristics, 8–9, 14, 24

plankton, 22
prey, 8, 10–12, 14, 26
R
reproduction, 20–22
S
scent organs, 16
sense of smell, 17
sizes of anglerfish, 8, 21, 24, 26
skeletons, 8
species of anglerfish, 6, 8, 24–27
T
teeth, 4–5, 14–15, 25

3 1524 00644 0020